Orphan, Indiana

AKRON SERIES IN POETRY

Orphan, Indiana

David Dodd Lee

The University of Akron Press
Akron, Ohio

Copyright © 2010 by The University of Akron Press

All rights reserved • First Edition 2010 • Manufactured in the United States of America. • All inquiries and permission requests should be addressed to the Publisher, the University of Akron Press, Akron, Ohio 44325-1703.

14 13 12 11 10 5 4 3 2 1

LIBRARY OF CONGRESS CATALOGING-IN-PUBLICATION DATA
Lee, David Dodd.
Orphan, Indiana / David Dodd Lee. — 1st ed.
p. cm. — (Akron series in poetry)
ISBN 978-1-931968-83-6 (pbk. : alk. paper) — ISBN 978-1-931968-90-4 (cloth : alk. paper)
I. Title.
PS3562.E3383077 2010
811'.54—DC22

2010012962

The paper used in this publication meets the minimum requirements of American National Standard for Information Sciences—Permanence of Paper for Printed Library Materials, ANSI Z39.48–1984. ∞

Cover: Photograph by David Dodd Lee. Used with permission.
Cover design: Amy Freels
Orphan, Indiana was designed and typeset by Amy Freels in Electra LT Standard, with Hypatia Sans Pro display. *Orphan, Indiana* was printed on sixty-pound natural and bound by BookMasters of Ashland, Ohio.

Poems in *Orphan, Indiana* have appeared in:
Barn Owl Review: "This is How It Sounds Before Real Things Start Happening" & "Saint Paul: A Hermeneutics"; *Field:* "1999" (as "I Can't Remember"); *Verse* : "Six Minutes" (online version); and *Zoland Poetry*: "Garlic Mustard," & "Civilian Defense, 1942".

Contents

III

IV

Heat stopped publishing 6 miles back
where the décor was a door hanging free from a hinge.
—Catherine Meng, *Tonight's the Night*

I'm speeding west somewhere in the top of Ohio or Indiana,
and to my right is the Arctic Circle, all white and scary.
—Arthur Vogelsang, A *Planet*

I

He Never Failed Strangely to Greet It

It all starts with the sentence, chain
of lakes like your blushing neutrality—

Houses in his little hand like dice

Then the windows reappear

I begin to pray in the dark

I stand up

Flashes of light like the moon

Headlights all over the highway . . .

Blood falls off the antlers

The suburb is smothered in rain coats

Smoke curlicues out of a red brick chimney

Nobody says a word

Not one of the other dreaming passengers

Antediluvian

In rows, as if injected by template

A Garden—
There is a symmetry to this plan that is unacceptable . . .

The flesh of her body
The flesh of the fruit

The most famous deleted page describes the "serpent"
Rolling downhill as a hoop, holding its tail in its mouth

five minutes till snack time

The snake tells the Missus to *Go for it*

He puts on Coldplay

The first-born son comes in October but his brother remains lost

Lightning—one-thousand one, one-thousand two—is followed by thunder

I should mention I have two missing wisdom teeth

Not *removed* from view—they never materialized

You couldn't just turn on the tap

She moved with him, grinding her hips

Sometimes I dream about groundwater

The Jammed Log Position

The trees' personalities become quantitative
at sundown

The hognose snake

Like the veins in her wrist

Lightly scored

I wanted to feel more real—the body of a lover

Night seeping into the boathouse

A calendar that doesn't go back

Cold, motionless well

Black nail polish

And then the thunder of a passing train

The sweetness of weeds

While the mercury bursts from its glass idea

Saint Paul: A Hermeneutics

Expect rain in the tri-state

Now buy a Slim Jim

We interrupt this program:

The Lord is the dead pen you shake back to life

They found him nailed

That rabbit in the lowing pines

Crying like a girl

This isn't the usual beach/woods stuff, an outer illumination

The father with his goose bumps

And terror

The sensuality of the melting Communion wafer

"dripping down the inner thigh"

(but enough John D. MacDonald)

The Jesuits walked home barefoot in the rain

They voted Paul off *American Idol*

I Would Sometimes Notice the World over My Shoulder

The law of gravity

or the Rauschenberg-like penalty of law

like noticing her eyebrows

the symbol in an elevator for *close door* suddenly taken out of context

I saw "Monogram"

and that goat had eyes in the back of his head

He had these empty hands

A man-made spine where there was never any love

The Bone Sculptures

You, you're undignified

like a logo

or high interest rates

Far from here, mint overpowers the must of leaf decay

Oxygen—

green as the inside of a glacier . . .

And the mist nets hang full in the understory, like Spanish moss

I like how you thought you knew everything

Ornithological

birds have no souls—we know that

they don't do much grieving

they can't write a check

or a detective novel

What the hell is this thing, and a wren pecks at a shiny table fork

It's almost 9:30

and I'm tired

I keep dreaming you and mother are trapped on a ship

surrounded by

a hundred other

burning ships

This Is How It Sounds Before Real Things Start Happening

I was eight again

Losses—I'll get him

A monarch squeaks squeezing
out of its transparent chrysalis

The windows blew out of our house that summer

We have so many shadows

A car burning in the Parthenon

Barbie with her head on backwards

I Have No Rear View Mirror and I Am Incomplete

Google this aerial view of southern Indiana

Why not

Insinuated like stitches in the wiring
of your cell block

Stud finders in a tool kit with dental floss

Your mostly over-examined

Petrified

Lilacs

The wind continued to bang one shutter

I couldn't drive north fast enough

Daylight saving time—

Subtract one hour from hangover

The Gentleness of Herbivores

Not enough landscape in your sleeping pill

that's one problem

that it was free, like heaven's enormous crybaby

Men

long neglected, stoned

super-attenuated

too much history in bourbon

too much Sepia Dream

his watch the size of a sundial, and the tassels

a bucket full of tip-ups

I prefer a cave that's cool and dreaming, a flooded removal

I met Larry Poons in an alley

and he gave me some centipedes

Now the deer talk quietly all night between raindrops

Everyone You See Isn't Everyone

The kid who played cornet

the serious
problem
that developed in the late sixties

with saddle shoes

I mean the fascist blight as echo . . .

the neo-incorrigible
codification of your basic Epsom salts

blood running over the beach

Arthur Lee

people slapping their children

I mean rods and aluminum bolts

All you need is an Allen wrench

wind

and an abandoned one-room school house

in northeastern Indiana

Poem for the End of Winter

They weren't dogs exactly

a citadel

something foaming at the bank

and me with no alibi—

fresh pencil shavings

I'd come across the cold water

huge beams of redwood with televisions bolted to the clouds

a dime flashed:

I had the great fish by the gills,
Freon pouring out of its eyes

I remember my mother, the instant she stopped dreaming—

like a circuit breaker—

three or four sparks in the bathroom mirror

Rapid Eye Movement

He said it wrong, the World

And like fire

The ghost of his hands, a laughable attrition

Falling and dying

Those first thirty seconds on a bike no-handed—

Somebody looks up

You could be screaming on a “northern corner”

No kiss on the breeze

That one collapsed vein

The sky *flatlines*—

They want to be birds

Beta-Carotene

Yes, I say, to the spirit world

A non-electronic intrusion

A whirl of leaves begins
spinning on a lawn
and moves through the street

It disappears in front of my car

Philip Glass on piano

Green tea spilling across the walls of the aorta

A fish begins thrashing in the toilet like a blindness in one eye

1999

1.
Twin loaves, or bees,
turn into butter . . .

the box turtle retreats to his lounge

he's a playboy

the serialization of friendly animals in advertising print has officially
 come to an end

Sebastian the scimitar

globes of primordial jealousy—

the organs purring
into substance

while it rains and the peonies rot . . .

2.
I failed there, in nautical heaven

too manic

sailing right past the buoys of ill repute . . .

I confess though

like yeast rising

it's the German engineering

Do you always wear black clothes?

I take a highway

I cross under a road I once lived on

The Wind in the Furnace

It's what you don't get to sacrifice

the worm writhing in the tequila

"imagination"

osteomyelitis

the way heat rises out of the flames in a furious rush

the X chromosomes blurring the face of the moon

detached retinas

glowing flowers growing backwards like a jar full of extracted teeth

and the sky that summer—nothing but bats

and the deck of cards left out on the screened-in porch

and the guttering candles

and the knife and the spoon with no fork

Christmas trees burning

cataracts

memory

II

Xanax

You can't split the time that way,
Before Coffin, and After Debt

even in daylight

The top half of the tablet is smiling

Cha-Ching!

it's like a lunar eclipse—

an aphasic in mourning

like smoke sucked into a giant straw . . .

Oh, I remember
I remember it fine

We played the harps, and then we beat them . . .

one hymnal per varnished pew

an ISBN for each bleeding knee

And still the births came

I'm thinking of a liver the size of a pencil eraser

I *choose* extra crispy

This is the migration of Eros

The Invention of Rope

Consultation green

the social evolution of the modern den floating on water

and the milk of the dreaming spider lily . . .

Endorse here

the pulse in his neck
the pulse in his wrist

the lengthening roots like an eel in his jaw

because of the damage to the hull his dreams were a compound

incompleted by spinal

(spinal deliberate

(spinal ignominious

the little key was as thin as a dime

her face an expression of fire

the air popped in each joint

he couldn't even say what was happening while the sunflowers swayed

moored there

living like the king of the underground

one exploding boat at a time

The Invention of Amino Acids

Criminal democratization

is not in the asparagus

But I know what you're thinking

re-charge golf cart

and

the indigo bunting doesn't even use a blow dryer

Spectator Sport or

Dream of Privilege

the back light in your mirror shows

a frightening display of deep woods

"woods"

The gardener whispers in the morning breeze

and that other wan metafiction

ectopic

The Calico Man

It's out there in the woods, north of Ypsilanti

"major and minor triage"

Grandiloquent of body-slam

The teacher made a noose, inside

And this is the composed, civilization

Procedure where the keyhole spits out sassafras

And all those other twilit diamonds shrinking to the size of a swimming scar

The body is a hinge

*

The Louisville Sluggers

I can't begin to tell you

They're eleven years old and he orders pin-stripes

What's left?

The Bomb Squad shows up and they cheer over the cyclone fence

Leprous contiguous

Although I can't see very well hiding under my bed

I mistakenly bought a first baseman's mitt

This is what else I remember:

The knobs of his dangling hand

Instead of a completion of fingers

Civilian Defense, 1942

(after Edward Weston)

She was gas-masked, darker
than shells

miles of coastal plutonium . . .

I'd rather you didn't

a cartoon landscape isn't a better idea

a cassette tape the size of a thumbnail goes into a slot
in the back of the manikin's head

"We're going fishing"

And all that other stuff, like royalty, hangs down in the rain

one arm falls off

"I've got some sandwiches"

I think of her eyes then

birds drifting sideways over blue Aleutian Islands' smoke

like drizzle misting over the grain elevators in Lima, Ohio

They just stood there
looking at the hotel bed

a transistor radio and static along with the pose

some kid must have gotten hold of the keys and gone crazy

Dominion of Insects

Yeah, talk into my hand

You, with your stone albatrosses

Your fat mind

I imagine marigolds blossoming in Dixie cups

But it was just your body in a Radio Flyer

Time to say Grace

I'd look at the fork
The spoon
The knife

We were that afraid

And the little four-legged rodents like pill bugs

White mice
And a pillow

Unraveling

I'd look up

You'd have this pound of meat loaf on your face

Outside the street lights were flashing

And the trains were derailing

What could we do with our naked arms?

Stunt Double

This is near Hanging Rock

Pole-stone and an escarpment where the poet undresses a girl

And what to do with half a human body

Make a chart on the wall

Nobody left to do all the carving

I mean nobody left to do all that kissing

He'd been remembering, inventing, taking notes

Stones in the heat aren't thinking but acting

It's the mystery of the missing twin

Boy-friendly

Carbonated with twilight

Inside Her Head He Has Another Head

It's because of the motion sensors in the floodlights

The universe bangs
like a hammered flag

In the middle of a sentence in English she switched suddenly to Martian

They sat talking in the quad

Sharing soy lecithin

My Lord, your boy is a sharp one

I'm afraid that is becoming the broader consensus

In Her eyes, His eyes

Their naked thighs in the breeze shivering, and parting, like menthol

Nature, hidden at the center of a coffee bean

I'm not kissing him again

Blue trees blowing to the music of Jan Hammer

She wants him to

He never stops thinking

The Neck of a Horse

Little is said then, her new hands

pale as the sand in the river

Six weeks in
and the creature divides

No skiff

the smell of burnt oranges . . .

She wonders about the dream

a fountain lights up like a translation snapping into place

Vitamin B in syringes

the tiny flat cakes of his nipples

The little ball shoots up tight into place on the trembling tube

she's panting

the stunted vines struggling through
broken stone all along the cobbled lane

an ibis flies out of the world through a missing manhole cover

she remembers the lake house—

washes out the memory with a hose

Black Diagram

My ten sisters lie face-up under their beds

To the sound of someone using a Water Pik

Cross your arms over your chest

And a giant red phone starts ringing on the other side of the glass

White doves flutter up where there used to be pillows

The jeweler takes his tweezers and plants a tiny Crucifix
inside each open window of the minuscule house

Now open your eyes

Solipsism

There's a long dream boulevard like an arm chopped off

chickens trampled in bone marrow

all this fog, and memory, pitching over the falls

the fish die in the mountains

each like a living fingerprint

I know this because I can hear her breathing

star-kissed and quiet as trees

the X-rays—

There's a translucent tube in the shape of a Y

she's pushed their blood through it

anchors bursting out of his broken fingernails

You open the museum door . . .

Poem Written in May

You don't want to die

Everyone talks around the secret of knowing

You might want to kiss a church

Naked bodies churning in the sunshine

I schedule what's next according to impulse

The removal of hair

Such discipline

Year holds a month holds a week holds a day

I don't want to think about 2021

Who I might be later on

Or was

That's my phobia

The Slower the Fan Blade . . .

You could be dying in a hospital

so far there
you're elsewhere

praying in the leaves, heard even through glass

the trees standing in the rain

good-bye

it is almost winter

the ladybugs die
and dry up—

wing shells pile on the alluvial plain

five days into November . . .

the brain, and the tongue
the spleen
wrapped in butcher paper

and the maple leaf spreads itself over your face like a human hand

a fish, with its red mind, waits under the shadow of an oar

Callisto, Ganymede, Io

Europa

Another shovelful and we're done—

The hereafter smells like the absence of ice

What You Take with You

I have no clear idea

the tongue

it's a monetary bastard

Frozen under
the heralding

of trees

from the Superior Basin

to the foothills

of Legoland

we're surely going to hell

In the ulterior
grace of God's

hinterland

the Sirens are given jobs in tanning salons

Odysseus
be damned

we did a 360
around that

billowing dream—

desire with its cock turning to stone

the moon

with its elastic blonde hair

In winter the ground freezes

Animal Magnetism

My analyst:
cheese curd capital of Wisconsin

a little levered
risible

"do you haf racing thots?"
as colonial as a matter of taste

(or Nature as entitlement):

take the
belletrist attitude—

pinpoint where a word became
the book you *loved*—

and shove it so the son
can't shine—

Dear Bruno S.,
It's like you can't grasp

the metaphor of these giant water bugs
dying in the author's

half-ton bed,
a hat that opens followed by a singing

H-Bomb—

And then it's winter—

Asbestos

Propane

Those same elephants once crossed these frozen plains

III

Garlic Mustard

It's invasive,

it cycles quickly through your information.

I thought then of the North Pole,

the sturgeon swimming in the underground stream,

the old freezer outside of Hastings hunkering in deep grass like a doorway to
 the underworld.

Sleep is a golden breeze all right

wheat still as the ocean under a geological moon.

And the weeds are absolutely choral, moving after the mind . . .

But now you're sequestered—

box inside a room inside a frame

(with that stink on your hands)

your wings breaking silver.

The carpet moth dreams in a pontoon zone.

He taps out a message . . .

The light hits all these icons that look like crabs, you see,

trojans or antibodies

croutons

and white flowers

drying, then crumbling . . .

And all you can do is grin through the bloodletting.

Kurt Cobain

A second time—

His second life

We make it all the way up to the space station

And look down at the planet earth

New cotton T-shirts for the newly dead

And Hazardous Waste

The problem of the lithium leach

Night is such a terrible time

The amnesiac awakes to what he's really done

2,000,053 dates on a Monday night

Corsage made of broken guitar strings

Only there's fluoride in the water

Toxic, in fact, to most Saints

Or you could be floating in an ethereal state

In a second cage made of stars

Feathers ripped

All over the lawn

All over the street

Weak Coffee

A little art, we get blurred corpses

A little art, we get dung on the Virgin

A little piss

Broken into pieces and violently smelling of gun powder and sliced apples

A little piss gets in the art

Chris Burden gets nailed to the roof of a Volkswagen Beetle

And I've seen how you flicker awake

Not born again exactly—

Not born into light

(You will never get to see Las Vegas)

But drowning into consciousness

(Where have you just come from?)

Surveys have shown people prefer a green landscape full of water and animals

They do?

The shaman of Nomenclature squeezes the shit out of the hypothalamus

He's aiming his flashbulb at you

He's dragging a bullwhip behind him

Writing

Are you really going to just sit there complaining?

This means everything you might think it means

I know

I see it, too

out there prancing on the grand promenade

but what gives with the self-deprecation?

Draconian Death Organ

(and are you cool enough to pull it off?)

Splenda then

a little injection

your poem, it really isn't so synthetic, or bad . . .

let's all put barcodes on our book covers

Vicky Cristina I Can't Pay to Get to Barcelona

I was in New York City in the rain with Herbert Scott

when a guy in one of those horse-drawn carriages yelled

"Make room for the little guy under that umbrella"

just rip off that normal face

Are you perfect enough for God?

Herb just laughed

Untitled Poem

And just what is a convertible-ized Winnebago

I'm sorry

The table is sprayed, fresh, capped with green soft drinks

Macaroni salad
and Georges Bataille

but I'm not sure what features come with the broken monocle

a teaspoon of S&M on your tuna fish biscuit

In the meantime

Get your television camera the fuck out of my house

(this isn't Elkhart)

Cindy Lauper mud wrestling

Larry Karaszewski

Zachary Zimbolee

(he's right in the phone book)

it's a bildungsroman

The story of a sputtering boy, and his dismantling of the learned, the too-
long beheld

and trust, preternaturally

"This is your blood speaking"

777 feet above sea level

Near Notre Dame

(May 17, 2009, South Bend, Indiana)

The landowner, and his girlfriend, were both standing on one leg

I was simply parachuting again

right on through the left side of the brain until I was almost with God

Deep, deep

the carotid is what the light shines on

the writ of habeas corpus

the geese, gentlemen

the geese

folding dark napkins

it was the most formal of floods, the Saint Joe with his toenail polish gleaming

and two miles away

the trucks with the body bits

coins and liquids

and politics

a crowd hushed under the dark night of all this spilling

I saw an oriole

rhythm guitar by Vic Chesnutt

the President stands in the university's carnival of animated light

some kind of plover runs over my left shoe

everyone's been ignoring my borders

The Unnameable Bone-Shell Room

Insect processes

everything stamen-inflamed to Fragonard

this is as it should be now

where there used to be a pond full of burning buses

a damsel on a swing made of gold ratchet wheels . . .

Could you be more frivolous

only if the dogfish ate and then spat out your pocket watch

it's as languid as Florida then

(ovipositor swelling between cerci)

The plumbing steams in both their chests

not a ticket for noise pollution

or evolutionary perversion played out

compelling analysis of the swinging-woman motif

who *should* be on top

Just put them in jeans, and let the 19-year-old wear his skinny tie already

(the cricket's not a violin)

the chiffon was swept up, separating the clipped-off wing covers

"L'amour est bleu"

It's somehow better that way

Mobile Home

I saw one with a chandelier crashed in the middle of the backyard

You might walk across the desert

Rooms opening and dividing before you

And never quite feel safe enough

I saw an abandoned one in Teegarden with a shotgun in the closet

I got lost in the forest there in the narrowest of hallways

Fire in all the trees for seven miles

In the seventies we were warned

The table was Formica and was tilted for effective removal of seeds

The snow fell for weeks without stopping

Whenever I strip a bed down to bare mattress

Graduation pictures and paneling

I don't know what's more cliché—shoes dangling from

An electrical wire or the wind blowing a Walmart bag against a fence

I saw a mobile home burning in a thunderstorm one time

Flames shot out of the small broken windows

The Romantics were singing "A Night Like This" on the radio

And the deer grazed casually in the field next door

I went home to my ground floor apartment a mile away and sat looking out the window at the rain and lightning until the sirens began

The Bliss-Tree Photographs II

We want it now—a room

Everywhere

Put Nature in a room, and be in it

Let your heart gush in a bowl

Roses

Blood pulsing out of the center of the chopped-up bed

Pull the axe right out of the wall

Start breaking windows

So the wind can get out

Sleep

Sleep as though you are completely willing

Until the idea of living just is

Six Minutes

The day eats itself then expires

Moths, dirty people

The animals match their blood to the earth and sky in that place

His face was the size of a pin cushion

Old lambs die young in this country

Programming Note

We should be able to summon that kind of blustery self-possession

The one, isolated head framed, and wind-whipped

The alabaster eyes

I remember standing in a west-facing hay mow

The sky divided by lightning into independent countries or states

A storm doesn't care about your little crunched feelings

Third-world world powers

The flat Mississippi mud on one large canvas multiply-cracked

And the rustling of dry cornstalks

Janis Joplin bleeding in neon while she binds her own wrists

We get Burt Lancaster leaping from pool to pool—

another day in the suburbs with John Cheever

(perhaps with your Tareyton burning)—

I can't believe I'm back in the sixties! some baby-boomer cries out

She's holding a vodka martini and laughing

He's thwapping a Blackberry against his palm and thinking *That bitch*

IV

Anamnesis

It double-tracks on you

The aquarium light

The turning

Of a swan-spun

Milked

Dream

Of perfection

This might be the tourism guide to the ghost
Boat of the postwar industrializing of diet TV

Like cavemen excavating a Woolly

Mammoth

And this isn't Before Time

Though it's before Casual Pleasure

Hot water running

In a luxury of silky cascades down one fairly oblivious

Blonde artist's

Shapely Euclidean ass

Dinosaurs did die and were buried

They turned into freight trains

No one anywhere in sight would ride them

Two-Thirds Cast Arbitrarily as "Mistress"

But mostly just talking about it

Each of us was given a kit full of thread and a mirror

Tools used for the occasional head exchange . . .

The narcissism

Implied, I mean

The genitals reacting in plain sight

We were

Secretly a product of our own initials

Like, *Who wants to play Gas Station*

(Nobody)

The panther only wiggles her tiny ass

The whole thing just grieves me

All those capital *Ls* and the tithing

JC with His shining crown followed by that bad boob job

Please Go Away

Lapse, *remember* . . .

We do a vertical pan

Shot through the sky like an abstract garden . . .

Stay right where you are

The Late Renaissance

I begin heading in the opposite direction

I like this song I heard on the radio about prostitutes fishing

One-hundred empty tollbooths in a row

Silence evolves

Just What Is It That Makes

Forty-eight eighty, a jawbone

a spiraling gate impaling the doe, who twitches in the moonlight

(Here is a bucket, now go find the leak)

the odometer looks over the carcass
and stops spinning

this is the mind-body connection right in your face

a hydroplaning stroll
through the cemetery

the glow of the bathysphere

the cosmos divided between theories of direct mastication

and the use of alien stones

but I only came to stop the applauding—

in one hand I'm holding *Little Birds*, by Anaïs Nin

in the other a copy of *TV Guide*

it's just nerves

You haven't even knocked and yet the door slams shut

the odometer begins moving again

the disembodied leg of a spider twitches beside a half-full glass of Dr. Pepper

Hunter's Orange

It's autumn—the Hendrix dies amidst the orange leaves

a car rumbles on

tympani

and the gun bakes in the lukewarm,
ventilated with paint

rufffffed grouse, the dog all asleep on his side

"I want to discuss overkill"

Or there's a tear in one eye

"You can't get through the foil and the cotton fast enough"

God's little love grenades

Reminds me of the time he threw the rabbit ears out into a snow bank

crows argue in the bright treetops

a spider mounts a box of shells (to the swelling of strings)

.410

double-ought

tuna sandwiches on white bread with one deviled egg

I push the tiller hard, and the boat shakes, luffing into the wind

"it's just a stress fracture"

it's just wildlife

Night Light

There's a crime scene near The Saint Joseph River

My point is, why are we still so obsessed with these penultimate leavings

Three empty nights on the beach

Something Catholic
sitting in a cracked clamshell

I'm not saying my night terrors are better than yours

You with that dental work

A cup of light in your hands you stole right out of Follain

I just can't stop falling in bed

It's like sitting at a red light crying

The hospital room looked so peaceful with the sheets pulled back up

Decorated with a light switch

Someone left a dog tied to a post outside the Dairy Queen again

Andalusian

We're spelling it all with bedbugs

Bon mot!

And then the drastic spasm
One might call his storming eyes

Believing, then belching

You and your paper people

"I'm coming to be near you!"

It requires elasticity to execute such a willful lack of dimension

And pedigree

And many layers of marketing know-how

That pulp is not ground chuck

Or screaming in a closet

You shake the love until the bruises leak out

No sunset for torture

Just rayon

And pigtails

I'll stick with Rolling Rock

Literally Himself in Spirit

(Dowagiac, Michigan)

The way we sit on the bus as if to say so

a cup with a few aspirin in it

one blessed blissful farmer who planted sunflowers along King's Highway

"Something keeps flying up top,
attached," someone said, "to the fuselage"

I don't remember the news exactly

One guy had eaten another guy's head I think

somewhere in Canada

or maybe he just hacked it off

"It's clinging with its sucker fins," is what our guy says

I say to the woman who has been knitting beside me for an hour

"Have you ever seen that *Twilight Zone* movie?"

It's easy to believe in God in the summer

Churches like boats
with no ceiling fans

My neighbor's got a cement pig next to his driveway

The knitter says, "I just graduated from Tulane"

good for you

Back about three rows a long-haired kid
cradles a violin case

He nods, and I nod back, look down at my book

(Carson McCullers)

Then there was the time in between heading south and nowhere

It was dawn

I was up

I don't know why

I just walked to the end of somebody's dock

It was early and dew was shining on the many spider webs there

Black widows all over the place

Dead Last in the Scheme of Things

(after Morandi)

Ill-traveled, last extant portrait uninflected taken in Moline

wandering over certain dark rivers

Where are we going after all, you wanted to ask

Nowhere in particular

The circus had come and it had gone

rings in the grass, a smashed almost smothered ethos festering on that far side of town

little white lights writhing up to the surface of things

other than that, the smell of petroleum products

"The bearded lady is waiting to hear from you"

everyone's a philosophical con-man

ladybugs all over the spandex, Japanese beetles all over the Queen Anne's lace

that bridge is a collection of notions and it got you safely into Illinois

Natura morta

and now this—

the whistling patriarch and his forty-year-old adolescent daughter in her
Underoos

the abandoned tenements standing in swamps outside of Gary felt abstract
with extinct business models and dead movie stars . . .

What's wrong with just *wanting* the chicken (to eat)

that throbbing in the knees for the hills and a mid-morning church service

not the IDEA of the circus

a painting to live by

five bottles, a tin, three boxes, one jug

that's all

Eligible for Aging

And so they take away the drinking hall pass

Just kidding

The hills between the transcontinental brain spheres . . .

More and more it's a relevant question

You wake up

Someone pronounces *Can't work on Sunday*

That's why the tongue is so willful

Might as well just lie down together . . .

Pink and protean

An autonomous muscle

Blind as a traveling clam

There's all this bodily putrefaction, and the sweating at night

Her salt, anxiety tinged with an excess of mental by-product

The doves swoop between pines

The lilacs keep blowing in a dream

The rest is just guessing

And the lizards slip through the dark from planet to shimmering planet . . .

But mostly we die not worrying

Snarge

Answer yes or no to the following questions

What if you were on the plane you are currently watching?

Yes

I am a cedar waxwing

Camouflaged as an arborvitae

There's a lot of fermentation going on this year

No

The goose enters this roaring cave

He doesn't have the appropriate documents

And for a second he's a monk in a hood

Smelling the rain on the dirt road

And in this manner we feel our lives are not so precious

We're tucked so safely inside

And it's really true

They do look like toys or little ants

Besides, everyone calmed right down after they piped in the Chuck Mangione

I am a pileated bushtit

The Bliss-Tree Photographs III

Thank you for stopping

There is a separate guest finger bowl in the nave of the motel proper

Drinking allowed

And the murmuring through the sliding reality wall

That's our tree full of insomniac bats

I see you brought children

You might want to take advantage of our wind tunnel to the subconscious

They really can't sleep

We provide conjectural biographies of Judy Garland and Pablo Picasso

The Screaming Woman with a Blue Guitar

Mascara dripping onto the little ones' backs

Our disposable biplane is available for exiting daytime or night

Just close your tired eyes

You may wish to remain supine while flying over the ocean

The red red mountains inland growing fainter and fainter

Government Sponsored

And he left that head near the Queen Anne's lace

Angling in toward a new chance for peace

That's right

But the doc doesn't get to peek inside until he gets cleaned up

Those were the days

Living gloriously week to week with no memory

Sometimes escaping to hide in the shade of another dumpster

Looking down through those wire rims

Sometimes the deer showed up at the check-in station already half stiff

I'd have to pry the mouths open with angle iron

And it was good to have such banged up wrists and be thirsty

I'd wake up walking over bridges five thousand miles away

He'd open the door and we'd sleep and we'd sleep

Forty Years Ago Last Week

Four of them maybe, thin little reeds with the appropriate fingers

We'd stand invisibly

Bangs touching the eyebrows, like Egyptians or terriers I said to someone
later on

The mandolin player entered the front door
And there were teeth embedded in the lead singer's shoulder . . .

A rather toad-like child appeared beside them and he was responsible for
vocal harmonics, like Art Garfunkel

This was on Castle Avenue actually, home of the wounded killdeer

Before my face became dwarfed with my father's endless exasperations

He would very much have liked to destroy a Jackson Pollock I think

I played the piano, then watched the record player for a while

The arm for the stylus moved on its own

"Now the man from La Mancha drinks too much," sang the mandolin player

That's why I left that theater and began collecting other beings

Like Roly Poly bugs

I found a Polyphemus moth dead on the grass one day like it was waiting to
be towed into a hangar

The creature both scared me and turned me on

But I don't mean it made me horny

I would sit in the grass holding my breath while a praying mantis slowly
turned to look at me

I had no reason to believe in anything else

Ice Fishing

There are thorns sticking out of my ear and one palm

Last night sank dreaming through twenty-three floors of pillows and classy
wallpaper

I picture one world where I'm breathing

Above the other within which I'd drown

You don't have to worry so much heading southwest in a long jagged diagonal
through the silence of corn

(listen, the wind stopped blowing)

My heart burrows up out of my chest and it is as cold as a willow

(there are too many guests)

The ice doesn't crack it *protests*

There are so many others I will never know

Astronauts, maybe

Far Away Home

It's night

And so the houses and trees seem to be moving

It's that still

Like music you can barely hear coming out of the groundwater

This makes me think of being lost amidst mountains
And forest, a white staircase or a beam of light

Heaven turns out to be a waterfall

The universe clarifies by degree

The farther you are from what scares you

Notes

The title "The Jammed Log Position" is taken from Forrest Gander's *As a Friend.*

The title "This Is How It Sounds Before Real Things Start Happening" is a line of dialogue taken from *A Hole in My Heart*, a film by Lukas Moodysson.

Some language in "The Gentleness of Herbivores" is taken from the work of John Ashbery.

"Animal Magnetism" owes something to Werner Herzog (and in particular, his movie *Stroszek*).

The italicized line in "Weak Coffee" is referring to an idea discussed in Denis Dutton's *The Art Instinct.*

In the poem "Writing," line 18 is from the work of Brenda Coultas; line 17 from a poem by Alice Notley.

Orphan, Indiana is for Louise Mathias.

Akron Series in Poetry

Mary Biddinger, Editor

David Dodd Lee, *Orphan, Indiana*
Sarah Perrier, *Nothing Fatal*
Oliver de la Paz, *Requiem for the Orchard*
Rachel Dilworth, *The Wild Rose Asylum*
John Minczeski, *A Letter to Serafin*
John Gallaher, *Map of the Folded World*
Heather Derr-Smith, *The Bride Minaret*
William Greenway, *Everywhere at Once*
Brian Brodeur, *Other Latitudes*
Jeff Gundy, *Spoken among the Trees*
Alison Pelegrin, *Big Muddy River of Stars*
Roger Mitchell, *Half/Mask*
Ashley Capps, *Mistaking the Sea for Green Fields*
Beckian Fritz Goldberg, *The Book of Accident*
Clare Rossini, *Lingo*
Vern Rutsala, *How We Spent Our Time*
Kurt Brown, Meg Kearney, Donna Reis, Estha Weiner, eds.,
Blues for Bill: A Tribute to William Matthews
Sharmila Voorakkara, *Fire Wheel*
Dennis Hinrichsen, *Cage of Water*
Lynn Powell, *The Zones of Paradise*

Titles published since 2003.
For a complete listing of titles published in the series, go to www.uakron.edu/uapress/poetry.html